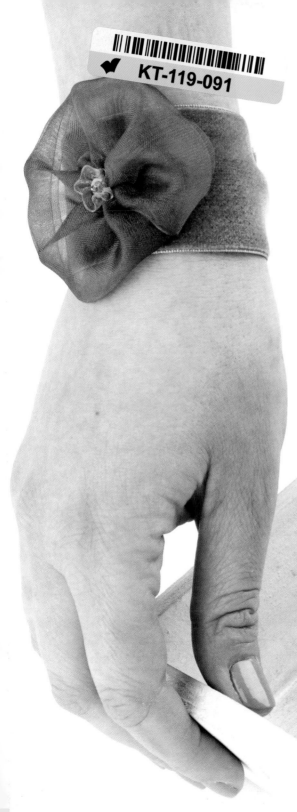

Contents

Introduction

All round the world, flowers are symbols of beauty and grace. From wedding roses to wild wood violets and from colourful, enthusiastic hollyhocks to tall, elegant orchids, flowers are always admired. While we can't always have fresh flowers, we can have a constant echo of their charm with a gorgeous fabric flower to perfectly complement whatever we're wearing!

This book contains twenty fabulous flowers, all easy to make and designed to suit all sorts of tastes and styles. Choose from pinked flower in fabulous fabrics to ornament a hairclip (page 40), a vibrant felt flower for your winter coat (page 24), a sparkling creation to pin to a clutch bag, plus many more. Attach them to shoe clips to make the most of ballet flats, to hats, to a bag to add instant detail, or to curtain tiebacks for interior style. You will need to add the required finding to turn the flower into the finished piece you want (see right).

You need no special skills to make the flowers and stitch instructions are included (pages 6–7). Where appropriate, templates are supplied. Simply enlarge them on a photocopier by the amount stated and cut them out. Many of the flowers need only scraps of fabric, so a raid of your stash will produce just what you need. Most of the flowers can be made in an afternoon, so there is no excuse for not having a corsage that perfectly complements the dress you are wearing that night!

Sew-on findings
Using a hand-sewing needle and doubled sewing thread, sew the finding to a suitably sized felt circle, positioning it off-centre. If the flower is made from substantial, opaque fabric and has more than one layer, use single thread and blanket stitch (see page 6), to sew the felt circle to the back of the flower, with the finding towards the top. If the stitches will show on the front of the flower, attach it using a craft glue that dries clear instead.

Stick-on findings
Either blanket stitch or glue a felt circle to the back of the flower, towards the top. Choose a strong, fast-drying glue appropriate to the materials you are using and glue the finding to the felt circle.

Permanent attachments
If the flower is to be permanently attached to an item (for example, a tieback or a bag), do not use a finding. Blanket stitch or glue a felt circle to the back of the flower, then sew the felt circle directly on to the item.

Twenty to Make

Fabric Flowers

Kate Haxell

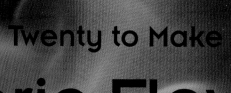

First published in Great Britain 2011

Search Press Limited
Wellwood, North Farm Road,
Tunbridge Wells, Kent TN2 3DR

Text copyright © Kate Haxell 2011

Photographs by Debbie Patterson at
Search Press Studios

Photographs and design copyright
© Search Press Ltd 2011

ISBN: 978-1-84448-699-1

Suppliers
If you have difficulty in obtaining any of the
materials and equipment mentioned in this book,
then please visit the Search Press website for
details of suppliers: www.searchpress.com

Printed in Malaysia

Stitches

Back stitch

Secure the thread on the back of the fabric. Bring the needle through the fabric and take a short backwards stitch on the stitching line. Bring the needle through a stitch length in front of the first stitch. Take the needle down where it first came through.

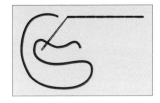

Stab stitch

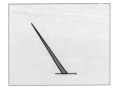

1 Secure the thread and bring the needle up from the back of the fabric.

2 'Stab' the needle straight back down, very close to where it came up.

Slip stitch

1 Secure the thread inside the fold of the hem. Bring the needle up through the hem and take it through just two or three threads on the back of the fabric.

2 Take the needle back into the hem, making a short stitch through the fold.

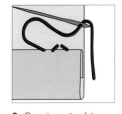

3 Continue in this way, pulling the thread gently to tighten the stitch, but not so hard as to pucker the fabric.

Blanket stitch

1 Secure the thread on the back of the fabric. From the front, take the needle down through the fabric on the stitching line. Loop the working thread under the point of the needle.

2 Carefully pull the needle through and tighten the stitch. Continue in this way, tightening each stitch so that a strand of thread lies along the edge of the fabric or motif.

Chain stitch

1 Secure the thread on the back of the fabric. Bring the needle through the fabric at the start of the stitching line. Take the needle back down right beside  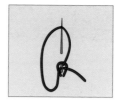 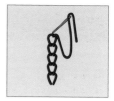 where it came up and bring it through to the front again at the end position of the first stitch. Loop the working thread under the point of the needle and pull the needle through. Adjust the stitch to make a neat loop.

2 Take the needle down right beside where it came up in the first loop and bring it up at the end position of the next stitch. Loop the working thread under the point of the needle and pull it through.

3 Continue in this way to create a chain of loops. Anchor the last loop with a small straight stitch over the end of it.

Lazy daisy stitch

1 Secure the thread on the back of the fabric. Bring the needle through the fabric at the centre of the flower. Take the needle back down right beside where it came up and bring it through to the front again at the end position of the first petal.

Loop the working thread under the point of the needle and pull the needle through. Adjust the stitch to a neat loop.

2 Make a short straight stitch over the end of the loop, then bring the needle up at the flower centre. Repeat to make as many petals as needed (usually five makes a good flower).

French knots

1 Secure the thread on the back of the fabric. Bring the thread right though at the position of the knot. Wrap the working thread twice round the needle and pull it taut.

2 Holding the wraps on the needle in place with the right thumb, take the needle back down right beside where it came through.

3 Still holding the wraps in place, carefully pull the needle and thread through with the left hand, pulling gently until the knot tightens. (Reverse if you are left-handed.)

Simple Flower

Materials:

Card for template

Two pieces of lightweight cotton fabric, one at least 16cm (6¼in) square and one 6cm (2⅜in) square

Fusible webbing

Sewing threads to match larger piece of fabric

Finding as required

Tools:

Compasses

Paper scissors

Fabric marker

Fabric scissors

Iron

Hand-sewing needle

Instructions:

1 Using the compasses, draw a 16cm (6¼in) diameter circle on the card. Cut this out to make a template. Use the template and fabric marker to draw a circle on the large piece of fabric. Cut out the circle.

2 Iron a piece of fusible webbing on to the back of the small piece of fabric. Using the compasses, draw a 6cm (2⅜in) diameter circle on the paper backing. Cut out the circle. Remove the backing and, following the manufacturer's instructions, iron the small circle into the middle of the large one, on the wrong side.

3 Finger-press a very narrow hem to the wrong side of the large circle. Thread the needle and double the thread. Knot the ends of the thread, leaving a short tail. Starting with the knot on the right side of the circle, work a row of small running stitches right around the hem, finishing with the needle coming through to the right side.

4 Pulling on both ends of the thread, pull the stitches up as tightly as possible and tie the ends of the thread in a secure double knot. Thread the ends into a needle and take them through to the wrong side of the gathered edge and trim them short.

5 Arrange the gathered hole so that it is centred on the small circle of fabric. From the back, make a few stab stitches (see page 6) through the puff into the gathered edge to hold it in place. Secure the thread on the back.

6 Add the required finding to the back of the flower (see page 4).

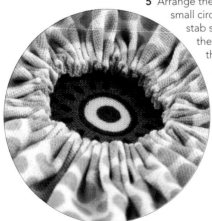

Feathered Silk

So quick and easy to make, these Suffolk puff flowers can be fun and funky, cute and colourful, sweet or stylish – it all depends on the fabrics you use. In this alternative, shot silk with a glittery linen centre produces an elegant flower that has a feather stitched to the back in lieu of a leaf.

Vintage Flower

Materials:

Card for template

Piece of lightweight cream linen
  fabric measuring at least
  16cm (6¼in) square

Strip of pink tulle measuring
  10 x 60cm (4 x 23⅝in)

Sewing threads to match fabrics

Decorative pink button

Stranded pink
  embroidery thread

Finding as required

Tools:

Compasses

Paper scissors

Fabric marker

Fabric scissors

Hand-sewing needle

Embroidery needle

Instructions:

1 Using the compasses, draw a 16cm (6¼in) diameter circle on the card. Cut this out to make a template. Use the template and fabric marker to draw a circle on the cream linen. Cut out the circle.

2 Finger-press a very narrow hem to the wrong side of the linen circle. Thread the needle and double the thread. Knot the ends of the thread, leaving a short tail. Starting with the knot on the right side of the circle, work a row of small running stitches right around the hem, finishing with the needle coming through to the right side.

3 Pulling on both ends of the thread, pull the stitches up as tightly as possible and tie the ends of the thread in a secure double knot. Thread the ends into a needle, take them through to the wrong side of the gathered edge and trim them short.

4 Arrange the gathered hole so that it is centred on the puff. From the back, make a few stab stitches (see page 6) through the puff into the gathered edge to hold it in place. Secure the thread on the back.

5 Fold the strip of tulle in half lengthways, matching the long raw edges. Thread the needle and double the thread. Knot the ends of the thread, leaving a short tail. Work a row of running stitch along the raw edges. Pulling on both ends of the thread, pull the stitches up as tightly as possible and tie the ends of the thread in a secure double knot to create a tulle rosette. From the back, oversew the short raw edges together.

6 Place the tulle flower behind the linen flower. Thread the embroidery needle with a short length of stranded pink thread. Place the button in the middle of the puff. Take the needle down through one hole in the button, through the fabrics and back up through the other button hole. Knot the ends of the thread together on top of the button. Trim the ends short and unravel them to make little tufts.

7 Add the required finding to the back of the flower (see page 4).

Retro Rosette

Choose pretty, soft-coloured fabrics to enhance the retro look of this simple but sweet flower. Here, aqua cotton organdie is used instead of the cream linen. This fabric has a lovely old-fashioned appeal that suits the style of the flower. Sew a pearl button into the middle of the puff using a cross stitch.

Embroidered Daisy

Materials:

Two pieces of purple felt measuring at least 10cm (4in) square

Stranded pink and blue embroidery thread

Craft glue

Finding as required

Tools:

Paper scissors

Fabric scissors

Embroidery needle

Small, stiff-bristle paint brush

Instructions:

1 Enlarge the daisy motif by 200 per cent and cut it out to make a template. Lay the template on a piece of purple felt and draw and cut out one flower.

2 Split lengths of embroidery thread into groups of three strands. Using one group at a time, follow the photograph to embroider the cut-out flower with a simple design in running stitches. Repeat in a second colour.

3 Sew the finding (see page 4) to the centre of the remaining piece of felt. Lay this piece on the back of the cut-out flower with the finding in the required position and make sure that all of the cut-out flower is covered by the finding piece of felt.

4 Using the paint brush, paint craft glue all over the back of the cut-out flower, brushing it right up to the edges of the petals. You will need to work quite quickly before the glue dries. Press the glued flower on to the other piece of felt, ensuring the finding is in the right place. Leave to dry.

5 Cut out the backing felt, carefully cutting around the flower.

The daisy motif shown half of actual size. Enlarge 200 per cent on a photocopier.

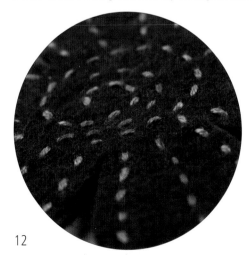

Bright and Beautiful

This folk-style red alternative flower requires only the very simplest of embroidery stitches to create a charmingly naïve effect. You can stitch any pattern of running stitches you like on to the felt, though generally it works best if the stitching relates to the shape of the flower in some way.

Button Flower

Materials:

Piece of medium-weight pink cotton gingham fabric with small checks, 15cm (6in) square

38mm (1½in) self-cover button

Embroidery threads

Craft glue

Piece of lightweight pink cotton gingham fabric with large checks, 55 x 10cm (22 x 4in)

Length of green ric-rac

Sewing threads to match fabrics and ric-rac

Finding as required

Tools:

Compasses

10cm (4in) embroidery hoop

Embroidery needle

Fabric scissors

Hand-sewing needle

Sewing machine

Instructions:

1 Using the compasses, draw a central 7cm (2¾in) diameter circle on the medium-weight gingham fabric. Put the fabric into the hoop. Use simple embroidery stitches to sew a design into the centre of the circle. Here, I have used three strands of thread in two shades of green to work a lazy daisy surrounded by French knots (see page 7) and cross stitches.

2 Following the manufacturer's instructions, cover the button with the embroidered fabric, making sure you position the stitched design centrally.

3 Using tiny running stitches in thread to match the ric-rac, sew the ric-rac around the edge of the button. Tuck the ends to the back and hold them in place with craft glue.

4 Machine sew the two short ends of the long strip of fabric together to make a tube. Press the seam flat. Wrong sides facing, fold the tube in half. Run a line of running stitch along the free edges of the tube, stitching through both layers of fabric. Pull up the stitches as tightly as possible to gather the fabric and secure the thread with a few back stitches.

5 Position the button centrally on the ruffle and arrange the gathers so that they fan out evenly around the button. Thread a hand-sewing needle with thread to match the button fabric, then double and knot the thread. Starting from the back of the ruffle, bring the needle through in line with the edge of the button. Take a small stitch through the fabric at the edge of the button, under the ric-rac, and then go back down through the ruffle. Work around the button in this way, sewing it firmly to the ruffle.

6 Add the required finding to the back of the flower (see page 4).

Summer Bloom

Gingham fabric is great if you are not a confident embroiderer, as the square pattern gives you a grid to work the stitches on. If embroidery isn't your thing, make a simpler version of this flower, like the turquoise one here, using a motif from a printed fabric to decorate the button. This bright, fresh-looking flower makes a great decoration for a summer bag.

Frayed Silk Flower

Materials:

Pieces of silk fabric in light and dark purple, each measuring at least 8 x 22cm (3⅛ x 8¾in)

Sewing thread to match fabric

Fusible webbing

Three pieces of green silk fabric, each measuring at least 10 x 12cm (4 x 4¾in)

Rayon machine embroidery threads to match silks

Piece of dark purple silk large enough to fit the embroidery hoop

29mm (1⅛in) self-cover button

Scraps of felt

Craft glue

Finding as required

Tools:

Ruler

Fabric marker

Fabric scissors

Hand-sewing needle

Paper scissors

Iron

Sewing machine

Small embroidery hoop

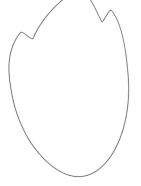

The leaf motif shown half of actual size. Enlarge 200 per cent on a photocopier.

Instructions:

1 Cut seven strips measuring 3 x 7cm (1¼ x 2¾in) from the light and dark purple silks and cut one short end of each at an angle. Pull out threads on both long edges and the angled short end to fray them, leaving the central woven piece of fabric measuring about 1 x 6cm (³⁄₈ x 2³⁄₈in).

2 You now need to sew the seven strips together in a fan shape. Alternating colours and the direction of the angled tops, overlap one strip about halfway over another. Using the hand-sewing needle and thread, oversew the square ends of the strips together. Overlap a third strip, sew it in place and continue like this until you have a fan shape.

3 Repeat steps 1 and 2 to make a second fan, changing the order of the colours and directions of the angled tops. Lay one fan on the other and oversew them together along the bottom edge.

4 Enlarge the leaf motif on this page and cut it out to make a template. Iron the fusible webbing on to the back of one of the pieces of green silk, remove the paper backing and iron the webbing on to another piece of green silk. Lay the template on the bonded silk and draw around it using the fabric marker. Cut out the leaf.

5 Iron a small piece of fusible webbing on to the lower section of the right side of the leaf and remove the paper backing. Lay the remaining piece of silk over the leaf and iron it in place; the webbing is acting like tacking to hold the loose silk in place. Set the sewing machine to free machine embroidery, fit a darning foot and thread toning rayon thread on the bobbin and top spool. With the right side (the loose silk side) down, use the needle to 'scribble' all over the leaf. Start with loose spirals all over the leaf shape (being careful not to stray beyond the edges of it) to hold the layers together. Then work over the surface with tight spirals and squiggles, sewing as close to the edges of the leaf as you can. Cut around the edge of the leaf, leaving a very narrow border of loose silk. Fray this with your fingers.

6 Using the template from the button kit, draw a circle on the remaining piece of dark purple silk. Fit the silk into the hoop. Using the free machine embroidery technique described in step 5, 'scribble' all over the circle using toning thread (I used a variegated purple thread). Following the manufacturer's instructions, make up the button.

7 Glue the frayed flower to the base of the embroidered leaf. Position the button so that it covers the base of the flower and bottom of the leaf. Make a small cut in the flower and leaf to push the shank of the button through. Cut one or two tiny scraps of felt, cut slits in them and push them over the back of the button shank so that it is flush with the surface of the felt. Glue the scraps in place, then stitch through the shank into the felt to hold the button in place.

8 Add the required finding to the back of the flower (see page 4).

Frayed Spray

Shot silks work beautifully for this project as the fraying makes the most of the different-coloured warp and weft threads. This alternative flower doesn't need any machine sewing. The leaf is two layers of felt joined with small running stitches in rayon thread. It looks really striking pinned to a coat or scarf.

Flower Choker

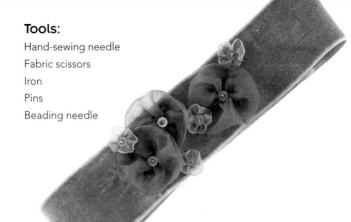

Materials:

Piece of pink velvet
  ribbon measuring the
  circumference of your neck
  plus 3cm (1¼in)

Pink sewing thread

Pieces of deep pink 4.5cm
  (1¾in) wide organza ribbon,
  10cm (4in) long

Pieces of pale pink 6mm (¼in)
  wide organza ribbon,
  5cm (2in) long

Beading thread

Sequins

Seed beads

Two poppers

Tools:

Hand-sewing needle

Fabric scissors

Iron

Pins

Beading needle

Instructions:

1 Turn under, press with the iron and slip stitch (see page 6) a
double 5mm (¼in) hem at each end of the piece of velvet ribbon.
Sew poppers to each end of the ribbon to fasten the choker. Check
it fits comfortably around your neck.

2 Fold the piece of 4.5cm (1¾in) wide organza ribbon in half
lengthways. Using matching thread, sew a line of running
stitches along the fold. Pull the stitches up very tightly and
secure the gathers with a couple of oversewing stitches.
Oversew the ends of the ribbon together to make a
simple flower. Repeat the process with the narrow
organza ribbon, but gather it up along one edge
rather than folding it in half.

3 Make three large and four small flowers and
arrange them on the front of the choker, with some
overlapping, to produce a cluster. Pin each flower
in place.

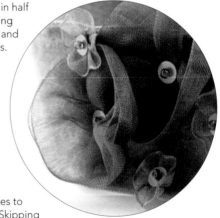

4 Using the beading needle and thread, sew each
flower to the velvet ribbon. Bring the needle up in the
middle of the flower and make a couple of small stitches to
hold it to the ribbon. Thread on a sequin and a bead. Skipping
the bead, take the needle back down through the sequin and the
choker and fasten off the thread on the back. Repeat to sew each
flower to the ribbon.

Rosy Wrist

This wrist corsage has a velvet wristband made in the same way as the choker, embellished with a layered flower made from very wide ribbon and very narrow ribbon.

Flower Cuff

Materials:

Two pieces of silk fabric, one striped, one plain, the circumference of your wrist by 8cm (3⅛in) plus 3cm (1¼in) all round

Scrap of dark green silk

Piece of fusible interfacing measuring the circumference of your wrist by 8cm (3⅛in)

Fusible webbing

Rayon machine embroidery threads

Hand embroidery threads

Two pieces of 2.5cm (1in) wide ribbon, each 25cm (10in) long

Tools:

Iron

Paper scissors

Pencil

Fabric scissors

Sewing machine

Fabric marker (optional)

Hand-sewing needle

Embroidery needle

Coin

Pins

Instructions:

1 Iron the fusible interfacing on to the middle of the back of the striped silk. Iron the fusible webbing on to the back of the scrap of silk. Enlarge the flower motifs on this page and cut them out to make templates. Using the pencil, draw round the templates on to the paper backing of the webbing and cut out the shapes. Peel off the backing and iron the flowers on to the right side of the patterned silk, following the photograph.

2 Set the sewing machine to free machine embroidery, fit a darning foot and thread rayon machine embroidery thread on the bobbin and top spool. Use the needle to 'draw' spirals in the middle of each of the appliquéd flowers, making each a different colour. Then 'draw' simple, daisy-like flowers on the cuff in different colours of thread. Place them between and overlapping the appliquéd flowers. Keep the embroidery within the area of the fabric backed by the interfacing; you can mark the area on the right side of the cuff with a fabric marker if you need to.

3 Using the hand-sewing needle and rayon thread, work chain stitch (see page 7) around the edge of one of the flowers and blanket stitch (see page 6) around the edge of the other. Using the embroidery needle and thread, add more hand-embroidered details. Try lines of running stitch on the machine-embroidered flowers and individual lazy daisy stitch flowers (see page 7).

4 Cut out the cuff: be aware that the stitching might have pulled the fabric in a bit, so check the measurements and draw straight cutting lines on the back if needed. With the cuff face down, lay a coin on a corner and draw around part of the edge to round off the corner of the fabric. Cut the rounded corner out with fabric scissors. Repeat to round off all four corners.

The flower motifs shown half of actual size. Enlarge 200 per cent on a photocopier.

5 Pin one end of a piece of ribbon to the right side of a short end of the cuff. Position the ribbon centrally on the edge, aligning the end of the ribbon with the edge of the fabric so that the ribbon itself lies along the cuff. Roll up the free end of the ribbon and pin it to keep it out of the way of the sewing to come. Repeat on the other end of the cuff.

6 Right sides facing, pin the plain backing fabric to the decorated piece. Make sure the pins go through the ribbon at each end of the cuff and slide out the pins originally holding the ribbon in place. Taking a 1cm (⅜in) seam allowance and starting towards the end of one long side, sew around the cuff, leaving a 8cm (3⅛in) gap in the long edge and removing the pins as you go. Trim the seam allowances to about half their width, then turn the cuff right side out through the gap. Make sure the rounded corners are turned out smoothly, press the cuff flat, then slip stitch (see page 6) the gap closed. Tie the ribbons in a bow to fasten the cuff around your wrist.

Oriental Cuff

This is a project the more experienced stitcher will have fun with. The simpler variation is made from oriental-looking flower print fabric. If you make clothes, make cuffs from leftovers of the fabrics for a perfectly co-ordinated accessory.

Naive Felt Flower

Materials:

Small pieces of cream and turquoise felt

Aqua crewel wool

Aqua button

Finding as required

Tools:

Fabric marker

Fabric scissors

Embroidery needle

Instructions:

1 Using the fabric marker, draw a small, asymmetric flower on the cream felt. Cut it out, then place it on the turquoise felt. On the turquoise felt, draw irregularly sized petals between the petals of the small flower. Remove the small flower and join up the petals to make the second, larger flower. Cut it out. Repeat this process using the second flower to make a larger third flower in cream, and then repeat on turquoise felt to make the largest flower.

2 Using the embroidery needle and crewel wool, work blanket stitch (see page 6) around the edge of each flower shape. Make the stitches irregular in length to add to the naive look.

3 Stack the felt flowers on top of one another, the smallest cream one on top and so on, in the order in which they were made. Use the crewel wool to make a couple of stab stitches (see page 6) through the layers to hold them in place.

4 Sew a button into the centre of the flower, using the crewel wool and sewing through all the layers.

5 Add the required finding to the back of the flower (see page 4).

Simply Beautiful

These freehand flower shapes can be as wayward as you wish, it just adds to the naive feel. This is a great project for a child if you can skip the blanket stitching. The brown alternative has blanket stitch on just some of the flowers, worked in suitably retro orange thread.

Big Felt Flower

Materials:

Card for template

Five pieces of felt measuring
at least 15 x 15cm (6 x 6in),
four in pale purple and one
in dark purple

Spray starch

Sewing threads to match

Small pale purple pom-pom
(one from chunky furnishing
braid works well)

Finding as required

Tools:

Compasses

Paper scissors

Iron

Pins

Fabric marker

Fabric scissors

Pinking shears

Hand-sewing needle

Tip:

When you are using pinking shears, it's worth taking the time to
match up the zigzag pattern around the edges of the circles for
the best finish. Make the first cut, then open the blades and line
up the pattern in the edge of the fabric with the serrations in the
blades before making the next cut.

Instructions:

1 Using the compasses, draw a 14cm (5½in) diameter circle on the card. Cut this out to
make a template. Use the template and fabric marker to draw a circle on each of the five
pieces of felt. Cut out the circles using pinking shears.

2 Following the manufacturer's instructions, starch the dark purple circle until it is very stiff.
Starch one side (the back) only. Lay the circle flat, right side up on the work surface.

3 Fold another circle in half then into quarters. Pinch the point of the triangle formed to
mark creases. Open the circle out to a half circle and lay it on the flat circle, matching the
pinked edges. The crease in the middle of the folded circle should be clearly visible. Pin the
layers together along the crease.

4 About 2cm (¾in) from the point, sew an arc of back stitch (see page 6) from the crease
to the folded edge, sewing one quarter of the folded circle to the backing circle. Finish the
threads on the back. Fold the circle back to a quarter circle, covering the stitching. Make a
few tiny and discreet stab stitches (see page 6) towards the point to hold the folded triangle
in place.

5 Repeat steps 3–4 with the other three circles of felt, working around the backing circle
and making sure that the folds all face the same way.

6 Sew the pom-pom into the middle of the flower.

7 Add the required finding to the back of the flower (see page 4).

Brilliant Bloom

Colourful and fun, the big flower is easy to make and looks great on a wool coat to brighten up the greyest winter day. As long as you use thin craft felt, these flowers also work well on a smaller scale. For the little bright pink one, the circles were 8cm (3$\frac{1}{8}$in) in diameter.

Net Flower

Materials:

White net, white tulle and silver net, layered and cut out to 15 x 55cm (6 x 21⅝in)

White sewing thread

Scrap of white felt

Scrap of fusible interfacing

Selection of silver beads, sequins, rhinestones and charms

Beading thread

Finding as required

Tools:

Ruler

Rotary cutter and cutting mat

Pins

Hand-sewing needle

Fabric scissors

Iron

Beading needle

Tip:

Net is not the easiest fabric to cut neatly. The best way is to pin the layers together and cut them out with a rotary cutter and ruler on a cutting mat. I used one layer of white tulle, one layer of silver net and one layer of white net.

Instructions:

1 Pin the layers of net and tulle together, matching all edges; treat the layers as one piece of fabric from now on.

2 Fold the net in half lengthways and pin the top edges together. Lay the net flat on the work surface with the pinned open edges away from you and the folded edge towards you. At one short end, put in a pin 2cm (¾in) up from the fold. From the same end, measure 20cm (7⅞in) along the open edges and put in another pin. Cut a gently curved line between the pins, cutting through all the layers of fabrics.

open pinned edges

cut curve

folded edge

3 Using the hand-sewing needle and doubled sewing thread, work a line of small running stitch right along the net, close to the folded edge. Pull the stitches up until the gathered strip measures 15cm (6in) long. Starting from the curved end, coil the strip around twice. Oversew all the layers together around the gathered edge.

4 Iron the interfacing on to the felt. Cut out two circles, each large enough to completely cover the hole in the middle of the net flower and overlap the edge by a small amount all round. Position the circles over the hole on either side of the flower and pin the layers together. Using white sewing thread, sew the circles in place with small stab stitches (see page 6) all round the edges.

5 Using the beading needle and thread, completely cover the front felt with beads, sequins, rhinestones and charms. Sew on larger pieces first, then fill in any gaps with smaller pieces and individual beads. Finally, separate and fluff up the layers of net.

6 Add the required finding to the back of the flower (see page 4).

Glamorous Touch

A fabulous, full-blown flower with a jewelled centre, this would look fabulous on a party dress to add evening sparkle. The simpler blue version is made with net with a stacked button centre, topped with seed beads.

Shabby Chic Flower

Materials:

Small pieces of fabric and felt

Grey and silver seed beads

Beading thread

Finding as required

Tools:

Compasses

Fabric scissors

Pinking shears

Pins

Beading needle

Tip:

When you are using pinking shears, it's worth taking the time to match up the zigzag pattern around the edges of the circles for the best finish. Make the first cut, then open the blades and line up the pattern in the edge of the fabric with the serrations in the blades before making the next cut.

Instructions:

1 Decide on the order in which you want the fabrics to be layered. Using compasses, draw a series of concentric circles, one on each fabric, from 8cm (3⅛in) to 3cm (1¼in) diameter, with the one that will be bottom of the stack being the largest. It is a good idea for this to be cut from felt to give the flower some substance.

2 Cut the circles out, some with pinking shears. You can cut freehand scallops around the edges of others, and it does not matter if these are not completely even. Using pinking shears, cut a small leaf from felt.

3 Lay the leaf on the largest circle so that the tip protrudes over the edge. Stack the rest of the circles on top, largest to smallest, and pin them together through the centre.

4 Using the beading needle and thread, sew a selection of seed beads into the centre of the flower, sewing the layers together at the same time.

5 Add the required finding to the back of the flower (see page 4).

Sumptuously Subtle

This flower offers a great way of using up lovely scraps from your stash of fabrics, and some petals are so small that even tiny treasures can be used. For the lacy alternative, a flower motif cut from a length of trimming is used instead of one of the circles, and peach bugle beads decorate the centre. Subtle colours create a sophisticated look.

Ribbon Rose

Materials:
Cream sewing thread

Cream satin ribbon 4cm
(1½in) wide and 80cm
(31½in) long

30cm (12in) of craft wire

Strip of silk fabric, 1 x 25cm
(³/₈ x 10in)

PVA craft glue

Tools:
Hand-sewing needle

Fabric scissors

Pasting brush

Knitting needle

Instructions:

1 Thread the hand-sewing needle and put it within easy reach. Lay the ribbon flat with one short end towards you. Approximately 8cm (3¹/₈in) from the end, fold the ribbon over to the right across itself. Fold it downwards over itself, so that the top forms a point pointing away from you and the working length of ribbon is lying parallel to the starting length. Fold it over again, towards the left this time, then fold it once more, folding it upwards. You should have a diamond of folded ribbon with the working length stretching away from you. Repeat the folds to make four diamonds stacked on top of one another.

2 Hold the stack together in one hand. With the other hand, feed the working end of the ribbon down through the hole in the centre of the diamonds. (You will probably need to nudge layers of ribbon apart to do this and the tip of a knitting needle is a good tool here.)

3 Still holding the stack, start to twist the working end clockwise. As the folds curl up to form petals, release them one-by-one and keep twisting the end until all the folds have curled. Avoid pulling down on the end as you twist it.

4 Holding the twisted end to keep the flower together, pick up the needle and thread and make several stitches through the base of the flower, making sure you catch in the starting end. Cut off excess ribbon from the working and starting ends and make more stitches to group the ends into a short stump.

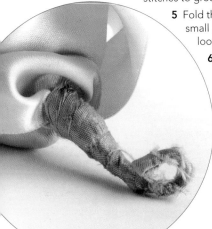

5 Fold the wire in half. Fold the open ends over to make a small loop and twist the ends around to close it. Sew the loop to the stump of the flower.

6 Paste some glue on to one end of the silk strip and wind it round the stump and loop, covering them completely. Leave to dry. When that section is dry, paste glue on the rest of the strip and wind it around the wire. Trim off any excess and bend the end of the wire over to hold the end of the strip in place. Leave to dry.

Fresh Roses

This is a traditional way of making a rose, and any double-sided ribbon can be used. The cream satin rose would make a gorgeous buttonhole for a wedding. The alternatives use beautiful organza ribbons for a fresh and delicate feel.

Pom-Pom Flower

Materials:

Card for circles

Torn strips of silk and chiffon fabrics 1cm (³/₈in) wide in two colours

Machine and stranded embroidery threads and eyelash knitting yarn in the same colours as the fabrics

Green felt at least 12 x 12cm (4¾ x 4¾in)

Sewing thread

Craft glue

Finding as required

Tools:

Compasses

Paper scissors

Fabric scissors

Iron

Fabric marker

Long hand-sewing needle

Instructions:

1 Using the compasses, draw two 10cm (4in) diameter circles on the card. Centrally inside these, draw 4cm (1½in) diameter circles. Cut out the two card ring doughnut shapes.

2 Leave the edges of the torn fabric strips frayed, but cut off any selvedges. If tearing the strips has turned them into thin, rolled lengths, iron them flat.

3 Place the two card circles together. Wind fabric strips and lengths of yarn evenly around them, as when making a traditional yarn pom-pom. Wind on layers of colours and threads until the centre of the circle is about half the original size.

4 Carefully holding the layers of fabric in place, cut around the edge of the circles, cutting through all the layers. Slip a doubled length of stranded embroidery thread between the two card circles and tie a single knot. Pull this knot very tight indeed, then tie a secure double knot. Cut off the card circles. Holding the tying threads close to the core of the pom-pom, fluff up the rest of the pom-pom and trim any too exuberant ends. The result should be a pom-pom that's flat on the side the tying threads emerge from.

5 Enlarge the leaf motif on this page and cut it out to make a template. Draw around the template on to the back of the felt using the fabric marker. Cut out the shape. Spread a generous amount of craft glue on to the right side of the central circular section. Firmly press the flat side of the pom-pom down on to the glue and leave to dry.

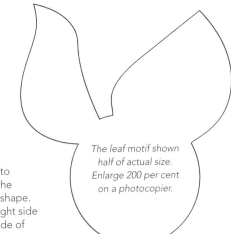

The leaf motif shown half of actual size. Enlarge 200 per cent on a photocopier.

32

6 Thread the long needle with sewing thread, double it and knot the ends. From the back of the circular base, take the needle up through the felt and through the core of the pom-pom, then back down through the felt. Make several stitches in this way, then fasten off on the back of the felt.

7 Add the required finding to the back of the flower (see page 4).

This is a wild and vibrant flower that adds a splash of colour and attitude to a dark winter outfit. It requires almost no sewing and is very easy to make. Children love making pom-poms and gluing, so it is a great flower for them to try.

Patterned Daisy

Materials:

Card for template

Five pieces of lightweight
   cotton fabric, at least
   14cm (5½in) square

Sewing thread

2cm (¾in) flat button

Decorative flower button

Delica or seed beads

3cm (1¼in) circle of felt

Finding as required

Tools:

Compasses

Paper scissors

Fabric marker

Fabric scissors

Iron

Hand-sewing
   needle

Tip:

You need a fine, lightweight cotton for these
flowers. If it is too thick, it will be impossible to
gather the flower up tightly enough.

Instructions:

1 Using the compasses, draw a 14cm (5½in) diameter circle on the card. Cut this out
to make a template. Use the template and fabric marker to draw a circle on each of
the five pieces of fabric. Cut out the circles.

2 Fold each circle in half and press, then fold each into quarters and press again.
Arrange the quarters in a circle in the order you want the petals to be.

3 Using the hand-sewing needle and doubled thread, work a line of running stitch
along the curved edge of one folded circle. Pull the stitches up as tightly as possible
to form a petal shape. Make a small securing stitch through the edge of the petal to
hold the gathers in place.

4 Without cutting the thread, repeat step 3 with the next circle of fabric so that you
have two petals strung together. Continue in this way until all five petals are gathered
up together in a strip. Sew the two ends of the strip together to form the flower.

5 Make straight stitches across the hole in the centre of the flower and pull them up
tightly to close the hole as much as possible. Make the stitches in every direction and
pull them up evenly to keep the flower shape circular.

6 Stack the decorative button on top of the flat button and sew them to the centre
of the flower. When making the last stitch through the buttons, bring the needle up
through one hole, thread on three beads, then take the needle down through the
other hole.

7 Add the required finding to the back of the flower (see page 4).

Pink and Peachy

For a simpler look, make the same flower from a single fabric and use a large self-cover button, covered in the same fabric, for the centre.

Ribbon Flower

Materials:

Four lengths of green 2.5cm (1in)
  organza ribbon, each 25cm (10in) long

Green sewing thread

Two green buttons, one smaller than
  the other

Delica or seed beads

Beading thread

Scrap of green felt

Finding as required

Tools:

Hand-sewing needle

Beading needle

Pinking shears

Instructions:

1 Fold each piece of ribbon in half and pinch the fold to mark it with a crease. Open the ribbon again. Fold over one end so it just overlaps the central crease, then turn that end of the ribbon over, so that the other side of it is against the crease and the loop has a twist in it. Repeat with the other end of the ribbon. Using the hand-sewing needle and thread, run a row of small running stitches across the crease, catching in both ends of the ribbon. Pull the stitches up tightly and fasten off the thread. Repeat this with every length of ribbon.

2 Stack the looped ribbons on top of one another in the shape of a star. Using stab stitches (see page 6), sew them together through the gathered centres.

3 Using the beading needle and thread, sew the larger button to the middle of the flower, covering the gathered centres of the ribbons. Sew the smaller button into the middle of the larger one. Bring the needle up though one of the holes in the button, thread on three or four beads (enough to fill the gap between the button's holes), then take the needle down through the other hole.

4 Using the pinking shears, cut two freehand leaf shapes from felt. Sew the ends of these to the centre back of the flower.

5 Add the required finding to the back of the flower (see page 4).

36

Beautiful Loops

Any double-sided ribbon works for these flowers, as long as it isn't completely floppy. Thinner ribbon makes a smaller, less flouncy flower. This alternative shows different shades of beautiful brown organza ribbon with a shisha mirror sewn into the centre for a touch of Bollywood glamour.

Velvet Ruffle Rose

Materials:

Two strips of green silk
velvet, one 8 x 25cm
(3¹⁄₈ x 9⁷⁄₈in) and one
8 x 30cm (3¹⁄₈ x 11¾in)

Sewing thread

Beading thread

Green sequins

Selection of faceted
crystal beads

Finding as required

Tools:

Pins

Hand-sewing needle

Fabric scissors

Beading needle

Instructions:

1 Fold a strip in half, right sides together, matching the short ends. Pin and back stitch (see page 6) these short ends together to make a circle of fabric. Repeat with the other strip.

2 Right side out, fold the smaller circle in half, aligning the raw edges. Using the hand-sewing needle and doubled thread, work a line of running stitch along the raw edges. Pull the stitches up very tightly to make a rosette of velvet with a gathered centre. If necessary, make stitches across the central hole and pull it closed, then secure the thread.

3 Turn under and slip stitch (see page 6) a narrow double hem along one edge of the larger circle. Using the hand-sewing needle and doubled thread, work a line of running stitch along the other (raw) edge. Pull the stitches up very tightly and secure the thread. The hemmed edge will naturally roll to the back.

4 Sew the rosette into the centre of the hemmed circle using small stab stitches (see page 6), through the centres of both pieces.

5 Using the beading needle and thread, sew sequins on to the central part of the flower, clustering them in groups. Bring the needle up through the hole in a sequin and take it down into the fabric to one side. Repeat, taking the needle down on the other side of the sequin.

6 Sew crystal beads into the centre of the flower, nestling them into the gathers.

7 Add the required finding to the back of the flower (see page 4).

Rosy Glow

This is a glamorous, grown-up flower that would look gorgeous on an evening dress or on a hat at a smart wedding. This alternative mini pink velvet rose can easily be made by gathering a length of 4cm (1½in) wide velvet ribbon, joining the ends and sewing sequins and beads into the centre.

Pinked Flower

Materials:

Pieces of light-weight printed cotton fabric

Spray starch

3cm (1¼in) and 1cm (⅜in) shell buttons

Craft glue

Beading thread

Seed beads

Finding as required

Tools:

Pinking shears

Iron

Beading needle

Tip:

When you are using pinking shears, it is worth taking the time to match up the zigzag pattern along the edges for the best finish. Make the first cut, then open the blades and line up the pattern in the edge of the fabric with the serrations in the blades before making the next cut.

Instructions:

1 Following the manufacturer's instructions, starch the pieces of fabric on the wrong side. Using the pinking shears, cut strips about 1cm (⅜in) wide and 9cm (3½in) long.

2 Fold each strip in half without pressing the fold and, wrong sides facing, glue the ends together. Leave the loops to dry.

3 Glue the ends of the loops to the back of the large button, arranging them to form petals. Leave to dry.

4 Thread the beading needle with a length of beading thread, but do not knot the thread. Take it up through one hole in the small button, leaving a long tail. Thread on a few seed beads and go down through the other hole. Pull the ends of thread tight and knot them securely on the back of the button. Glue this button into the centre of the large button.

5 Add the required finding to the back of the flower (see page 4).

Fifties Chic

This no-sew flower is quick and simple to make. It's a great project for a child to do,
but small children should have the fabric strips starched and cut for them.
For the bright variation, strips of boldly striped fabric and a couple of vintage
buttons make a flower with a retro 1950s feel.

Buttonhole Flower

Materials:

One piece of wired-edge ribbon 3.5cm (1⅜in) wide by 25cm (9⅞in) long

Matching sewing thread

Piece of green fabric, 15 x 7cm (6 x 2¾in)

Button

PVA glue

Soft craft wire 10cm (4in) long

Finding as required

Tools:

Pins

Hand-sewing needle

Iron

Pasting brush

Wire cutters

Fabric scissors

Instructions:

1 On one edge, carefully push the ribbon back a little way along the wire. Fold the end of the wire over to prevent it slipping inside the edge of the ribbon. Repeat at the other end of the same edge.

2 On the other edge, push the ribbon back along the wire on both ends until you can firmly grasp the wire. Holding both ends of the wire, push the ribbon up along it until it is as tightly ruffled as it can be. Twist the ends of wire firmly together and cut off the excess.

3 Pin the short, cut ends together, matching the top (ungathered) edge of the ribbon. Using the hand-sewing needle and thread, back stitch (see page 6) the ends together, taking a very small seam allowance. If the ribbon frays a lot, oversew the seam allowance.

4 Sew a button into the centre of the flower.

5 Fold the strip of green fabric in half widthways and press the fold, then open it out flat again. Make a tiny loop in one end of the soft craft wire. Cover the fabric on one side of the crease with a thin layer of PVA glue. Lay the wire on the glue, at right angles to the crease, with the loop about 5mm (¼in) from the crease. At the crease, fold the other end of the fabric over on to the glued fabric. Press the layers firmly together and leave for five minutes.

6 Cut a freehand leaf shape from the fabric, with the wire as the central stem. If you prefer, you can draw on an outline first. Bend the wire and shape the fabric to make a curved leaf and leave it to dry completely.

7 Bend the free end of the wire into a small loop and cut off any excess. Oversew this loop to the back of the centre of the flower.

8 Add the required finding to the back of the flower (see page 4).

Wedding Finery

This is a smart, but not too formal, flower that makes a perfect buttonhole for a contemporary wedding. There are lots of different wired ribbons available. Choose checked or striped designs for the boys, and something more feminine for girls. This one is a pretty organza flower with a beaded middle and a silk leaf.

Organza Rose

Materials:

Two pieces of dark pink
    organza fabric measuring
    10 x 10cm (4 x 4in)

Two pieces of medium pink
    organza fabric measuring
    8 x 8cm (3$^1/_8$ x 3$^1/_8$in)

Two pieces of light pink
    organza fabric measuring
    6 x 6cm (2$^3/_8$ x 2$^3/_8$in)

Matching beading thread

Silver seed beads

Finding as required

Tools:

Fabric sciss

Beading ne

Tea light

Tip:

I bought short lengths of organza ribbon of
different widths as this saved me having to buy
quite a lot of fabric in order to make just one
flower. However, if you are making multiple
flowers, it is better value to buy fabric.

Instructions:

1 One by one, fold the squares of organza into quarters, then fold each quarter in
half diagonally, and cut a deep curve across the open ends. Open each piece out
to reveal a rough flower shape. The shapes can be completely irregular – it only
adds to the vintage effect. Make four short snips at the main points of the compass
towards the centre of each flower shape.

2 Practise this next step on scraps of organza before you start on the project pieces.
Light the tea light. Very carefully hold the edge of an organza petal towards the
flame. As it gets close to the heat, the edge of the fabric will start to melt and curl
up. Be careful, you don't want the edge to burn or the fabric to catch light. Turn the
flower shape to melt the edge all the way around. Repeat for every flower shape.

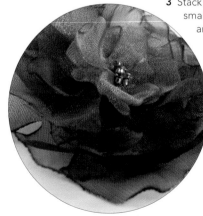

3 Stack the flowers on top of one another, the
smallest on the top. Thread the beading needle
and make a couple of tiny stab stitches (see
page 6) through all the layers to hold the
stack together. Work a small circle of
running stitch round the central holding
stitches and pull them up very tight to
ruffle the flower a bit. Make several
securing stitches through the gathers on
the back.

4 Sew seed beads in a tightly clustered
group at the centre of the flower.

5 Add the required finding to the back of
the flower (see page 4).

English Rose

This is a pretty, vintage-style rose that's simple to make. It does involve using a candle, so this isn't a project for children. The alternative flower doesn't have the snips going in towards the centre, so it has more of an old English, cabbage rose look. The petals are all one colour and a tiny pearl button gives a sweet touch.

Folk Flower

Materials:

Two pieces of lightweight fusible interfacing, each 12 x 12cm (4¾ x 4¾in)

Four pieces of red linen fabric, each 12 x 12cm (4¾ x 4¾in)

Red sewing thread

Red rayon machine embroidery thread

Small pearl four-hole button

Finding as required

Tools:

Paper scissors

Iron

Pins

Fabric marker

Fabric scissors

Sewing machine

Hand-sewing needle

Instructions:

1 Enlarge the motif on this page and cut it out to make a template. Iron fusible interfacing on to the back of one piece of fabric. Lay the template on the interfacing, draw around it and cut out a flower.

2 Interfacing side down, pin the flower to the wrong side of another piece of fabric. Set the sewing machine to a narrow satin stitch. Put the fabric under the machine, flower (wrong) side up. Satin stitch right around the edge of the flower, stitching the layers together.

3 Turn the flower over. Setting the machine to different stitch widths for every line, satin stitch straight lines radiating out from the centre to the dips between petals. Take the ends of threads through to the back and fasten them off.

4 Cut out the flower around the edge, cutting as close as possible to the stitching without cutting into it. Make a second flower in the same way, but without the radiating satin stitch lines.

5 Stack the flower with lines on top of the plain one, arranging them so that the petals are misaligned. Using the hand-sewing needle and red thread, sew the button into the centre of the flower, sewing the layers together at the same time. Make stitches in a cross shape and then in a square to fill the middle of the button with colour.

6 Add the required finding to the back of the flower (see page 4).

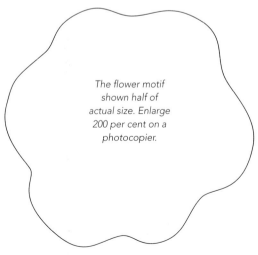

The flower motif shown half of actual size. Enlarge 200 per cent on a photocopier.

Lovely in Linen

These are great flowers to make if you're not keen on hand sewing as they are almost entirely done on the machine. This stylishly simple, subtly coloured alternative has a modern craft feel to it.

Acknowledgements

My thanks to the team at Search Press,
especially Sophie Kersey, and to
Debbie Patterson, for their work
on this book.

You are invited to visit the
author's website
www.katehaxell.co.uk

Publisher's Note
If you would like more information about sewing and
textiles, try *Twenty to Make Bunting and Pennants* also
Kate Haxell, Search Press, 2011 or *Sew Scandinavian* b
Nadja Knab-Leers & Heke Roland, Search Press, 2010